let's **talk** ab

Toys

D1461523

Published 2010 by A&C Black Publishers Limited
36 Soho Square, London W1D 3QY
www.acblack.com

ISBN 978-1-4081-2667-7

Text © Keri Finlayson 2010
Design © Lynda Murray
Photographs © Fotolia
Cover photos © Shutterstock 2010
A CIP record for this publication is available from the British Library.

Printed in Great Britain by Latimer Trend & Company Limited

This book is produced using paper that is made from wood grown
in managed, sustainable forests. It is natural, renewable and
recyclable. The logging and manufacturing processes conform to
the environmental regulations of the country of origin.

To see our full range of titles visit
www.acblack.com

Contents

The 'Let's talk about' series

Communication is vital. The ability to communicate and the ability to comprehend are the most important skills we can foster in young children. Without the ability to speak clearly, listen carefully, and comprehend fully a child's ability to develop literacy and numeracy, and to understand the world around them is compromised.

The 'Let's talk about' series reflects the aims of the Every Child a Talker initiative and promotes verbal communication skills within an environment where children can enjoy experimenting with language. It aims to give those who work with children in the early years, tools for phonological instruction and to offer entertaining, exciting and stimulating activities that foster early language learning. Each book focuses on a popular Early Years theme. The theme is used throughout the book, allowing the practitioner to create a day's activity or a week or term long project.

Speaking and listening are skills that are essential for the development of reading and writing. The ability to articulate clearly is extremely important when acquiring, developing and understanding spoken and written language. The clear and correct pronunciation of words enhances a child's phonological awareness (the ability to distinguish the sounds that make up words) and this in turn promotes the understanding of spelling patterns that will be an essential part of literacy success later on.

Communication Matters: Strands of Communication and Language (DfES 2005) states that:
"There is much variation in the ages in which children who are developing normally learn about features of communication and language. As they are learning, they will also tend to concentrate on particular things at particular ages. So, in infancy they concentrate on the sound patterns of the language; as toddlers they focus on learning words and putting them together; and as young children they learn to extend their proficiency as communicators in a wide range of situations. However, although they might concentrate on different things at different times each is important throughout."

The 'Let's talk about' series has been designed with this development across and within strands in mind, and will encourage children to:

- Know and use sounds and signs.
- Know and use words.
- Structure language.
- Make language work.

Using this book

In this book you will discover games that get tongues twisting and lips smacking! There are activities that teach creative communication and foster creative expression, and short plays in age appropriate language that encourage children to become confident and clear communicators. Most of the activities involve lots of chatter and some involve lots of noise!

The activities are suitable for small groups of children, as well as whole class groups. Children have varying attention spans, development rates and areas of interest. You can lengthen, shorten or adapt the activities according to your professional judgement.

The topic of toys provides the early years practitioner with a wealth of ideas. It covers a wide range of early learning goals in areas from Literacy and Numeracy to Knowledge and Understanding of the World. Toys are an integral part of a young child's life and learning. Toys can be used in role-play situations, allowing children to explore topic-based vocabulary. Toys are used in games, giving children a focus for instructional talk. And most importantly, toys can be friends and confidents, providing opportunities for intimate talk.

Communication friendly settings

Creating the right environment

Early years practitioners know how important it is to create a setting that encourages children to communicate with each other and with the adults who look after them. This is not always easy in the hustle and bustle of an early years setting. There are many demands on a practitioner's attention and children often raise their voices to be heard or rely on physical cues to communicate needs. By creating a word-sound-rich environment where word sounds are readily heard, children learn that spoken words can do many things. They learn that spoken words convey instructions, describe the physical world around them, and that spoken language enables them to describe their own thoughts feelings, needs and wants.

Developing language and listening skills are fostered by creative exploration and play. Language games, storytelling, dialogic reading, poetry and performance are all excellent ways of doing this and the environment in which these activities take place is very important.

In this section you will find suggestions on how to create an environment that will:

✓ Foster, extend and explore spoken language in your setting.

✓ Encourage confident and articulate conversations between children.

✓ Foster listening and aural discrimination skills.

✓ Allow children to feel relaxed and confident with their speech.

The ideas in this section, as is in the rest of the book, are based around the theme of toys but they can be adapted to suit your needs and preferences.

Some general tips and suggestions

Talking together

Speaking and listening well is not just something we encourage children to do – it is something we must also do well ourselves. This isn't always easy in a busy early years setting, but early years practitioners know that they are role models for active listening and active learning. The way in which we speak to children who are beginning to develop language is vital.

Remember to:

★ **Be seen**

Children need to be able to see our faces and to hear our voices clearly. When speaking to a young child it's important to bend or kneel down if possible. Keep a small cushion near by to kneel on when talking; it could save your knees and your back!

★ **Be expressive**

If your face is lively and animated then you will communicate enthusiasm to the children and they will watch your face closely. The children you are talking to are absorbing the way you form words and are learning new vocabulary all the time.

★ **Be focused**

Make sure that speaking is the only task you are performing. It is easy to slip into the habit of speaking while engaged in another task, such as marking, recording, reading, or even using a computer. It is vitally important that communication is always the priority.

Making conversation – the practitioner as model

Conversation is at the heart of speaking and listening. We all enjoy a friendly, funny, or informative conversation, and we all appreciate it when a conversation is well mannered. As a practitioner you are able to show the children in your care how to conduct a conversation well by:

- Showing genuine interest in what a child tells you.
- Asking a question to follow up what a child has said.
- Adding a fact about your own views or interests.
- If a child asks you a follow up question, expressing pleasure in the fact that they have shown an interest in you.
- If you feel a child wants to talk at length, one to one, try to make time to do this.

Being a good listener

Encourage your children to identify and articulate what makes a good listener and a good speaker themselves. By reflecting on what makes for good speaking and listening and then sharing their thoughts with a group, a child develops a sense of ownership over the task. By identifying problems or difficulties themselves, a child can focus on improving their own skills and assisting

others with theirs. Good speaking goes hand in hand with good listening. By listening carefully children learn to:

- Follow instructions.
- Comprehend what is happening around them.
- Appreciate what is expected of them.
- Understand the thoughts and perspectives of others.
- Learn information.
- Learn language structure and vocabulary.
- Make friends.

Dealing with interruptions

There are many ways of teaching children not to interrupt or call out and most practitioners develop their own techniques. Raising a hand and then speaking when given permission to do so is the most popular where groups of children are involved. This is a tried and tested method and works well. However, it is obviously not appropriate in all contexts. Imagine if you were asked to raise your hand before speaking during a dinner with friends or while having a conversation with a shopkeeper!

Try using 'Cock-a-doodle the interrupting cockerel' to demonstrate the effect interrupting has on others so that children understand the reason why we raise our hands when talking

cock-a-doodle-doo!

in a group, or why we allow others to finish speaking before we start. All you need is a cockerel puppet/toy that interrupts you when you are talking with a loud cock-a-doodle-doo! Show how irritated you are with his interruptions and ask him to stop and the children will soon begin to understand what you are talking about!

Making special places

Creating screened off or enclosed spaces for talk, allows children to develop scenarios without distraction and to practise important conversation skills. This can be tricky if your setting is a pack-away one in a large open space such as a hall. If your setting doesn't naturally lend itself to private spaces you could:

- Screen off a corner by draping a sheet over two chairs and pegging them in place.

- If you are able, fix two hooks on to the two walls that form a corner, stretch a wire or string (well above head height) from the hooks and drape a sheet over it (fixed with clothes pegs).

- Purchase or borrow pop up play tents or beach tents that can be placed anywhere in the setting.

- Collect large cardboard boxes and stack them to form special places.

- Tables can be sat under – cover with a large sheet to create more privacy. (Don't put anything on top of the table that could fall on a child if the sheet is pulled down.)

- Large sheets of cardboard can be leant against a wall to create a 'lean to'. Place a box of books at the base to stop it slipping down.

- Use boxes of books to mark off a corner space.

- Young children are adept at creating their own private spaces or dens. Offer them sheets, boxes and plastic clothes pegs and see what they come up with themselves!

- See also the *A Place to Talk* series by Featherstone for lots more ideas on creating communication friendly spaces.

Storytelling and story making areas

Children learn so much from listening to stories. You can enhance their experience by creating special spaces for storytelling and story making. Make a space that can be transformed in minutes into a calm place for focused listening and then into a stimulating environment for retelling and narrative based play.

Story time traditionally is an activity that takes place at the end of a session. Try telling a story at the beginning of a session to directly inspire play. Provide props and costumes that relate to the story then encourage some children to stay in the story space while you withdraw.

De-clutter, re-clutter

De-clutter your story space so it doesn't distract from the narrative. When you are telling a story all eyes should ideally be on you. Make focusing easy for little listeners by minimizing visual distractions.

Re-clutter the space with relevant materials to prompt retelling or narrative based play. Place chosen material in the area after you have finished telling the story. Children can then use the materials as props and prompts to retell the story or engage in role-play.

Keep it quiet

Early years settings are noisy places, with plenty of laughter, shouts, bangs and crashes. However, during story time, make sure that the only sounds heard are the voices of those telling the story. Minimize noise levels by either telling a story to the whole group or by engaging non-story listening children in quieter activities.

Spaces for small world play

Small world toys provide endless opportunities for talk. While playing with small world scenarios children can:

- Explore scenario-focused vocabulary.
- Conduct off topic conversations with other children engaged in the play.
- Use talk to direct the play.
- Use talk to voice the characters being played with.
- Use talk to negotiate the direction of the play.

Small world play can take place in any space, but providing children with an enclosed or defined space where their world can unfold allows them to focus on the scenario they are exploring. Proximity (close play) fosters conversation and verbal negotiation. Try the ideas on the following pages for contained spaces that promote conversation.

Links *for all small world activities*

CLL LfC. 40+m
- Interact with others, negotiating plans and activities and taking turns in conversation. (ELG)

CD DI&IP. 40+m
- Play alongside other children who are engaged in the same theme.

PSED D&A. 40+m
- Persist for extended periods of time at an activity of their choosing.

Make your own playmats

Playmats are available commercially, but can be created, with the children's help, to suit your topic. These simple cardboard playmats encourage children to discuss the creation of a world and to negotiate its layout.

What you do

- Cut the cardboard box so that it lies flat. It doesn't have to be a regular shape when flat – the flattened sides and lid add interest.
- Discuss what the mat is going to be. Will it have roads? Houses? Will there be a park? Is there a pond?
- Ask a small group of children to draw the small world themselves.
- Add the toys to the world and allow the play to unfold.
- Provide more cardboard if the children want the world to expand.
- Make sure that the cardboard is placed on a protective covering so that crayon roads do not wander over flooring!

What you need

- ✓ Large cardboard boxes
- ✓ Scissors
- ✓ Large crayons
- ✓ Small world toys as appropriate

Another idea

Provide a box of junk card (mini cereal boxes, tubes, etc) so that 3D buildings can be added to the world.

Chalk talk

Large chalk is excellent for creating a play world outside. Show the children how to draw houses, towns, roads and forests and let their imaginations and hands run wild. Keep a pot of chalks alongside the play. This allows for the scenario and play space to expand and develop as children discuss their new world.

What you do

- Take the children outside and sit them in a circle.
- Model the creation of a chalk world in the centre of the circle.
- Draw a circle and say, "This is a house. Who do you think lives here?"
- Ask a child to choose a toy to live in the house.
- Draw a line from the house to represent a road that can lead to another house.
- Ask for suggestions. "What else could be in the chalk world?"
- Provide a pot of large chalks and a set of small world toys for a group of children then let them create their own world.
- Stress that drawing on walls and floors should only be done outside and only with chalk.

What you need

- ✓ An outside space
- ✓ Large chalks
- ✓ Small world toys as appropriate

Communication friendly settings

Puppets - talking with toys

Talking with toys and talking as toys.

- Playing with puppets allows children to give voice to their own thoughts and feelings.

- Playing with puppets provides opportunities to talk with somebody and to talk as somebody.

- Puppets allow children to explore other voices and inhabit other characters.

- Puppets allow children to create monologues (talking by themselves), dialogues (talking with someone else) or to give voice to characters in group play.

- Puppets can be used to reenact a story or rhyme.

- Children often feel comfortable talking to puppets about subjects that concern them.

Have a variety of puppets available in your setting. Provide children with a range of characters so they can explore a range of personalities and topics. Try the following ideas (pages 12-15) to create your own characters.

Links *for all puppet activities*

CLL LfC. 30-50m

- Use vocabulary focused on objects and people that are of particular importance to them.

- Build up a vocabulary that reflects the breadth of their experiences.

- Describe main story settings, events and principal characters.

- Use a widening range of words to express or elaborate on ideas.

Lolly stick puppets

Lolly sticks are useful for creating simple families of characters. They can be used to act out scenarios or stories.

What you need

- ✓ Clean wooden lolly sticks
- ✓ Stiff card
- ✓ Felt pens
- ✓ PVA glue
- ✓ Fabric scraps
- ✓ Wool strands
- ✓ A shoebox or similar

What you do

- Decide on the characters you want to create. These can be from a favourite fairy tale, a nursery rhyme or even from a film or television programme.
- Cut a circle of card to create a face and draw features.
- Add wool strands for hair.
- Glue the face to the top of the lolly stick.
- Colour in the body of the stick using the felt pens.
- Cut and glue fabric scraps to make clothing.
- Store characters in a labeled shoebox.

Block puppets

Wooden blocks make excellent character puppets for story retelling. You can make the scenery and props too. Use them to retell your favourite story.

What you need

- ✓ A variety of wooden blocks, cubes and cuboids.
- ✓ Glue
- ✓ Felt
- ✓ Scissors
- ✓ Storage box

What you do

- Choose characters or a story to create.
- Draw out simple images for the characters.
- To make a king use:
  - Yellow felt crown
  - Pink circle for face
  - Purple triangle for cloak
- To make a tree use:
  - Small brown rectangle for trunk
  - Green oval for leaves
- Cut out the felt shapes.
- Glue to one face of your wooden block.

Pillow puppets

Children often confide in their toys and enjoy conducting private soliloquies. These private monologues are an important part of language acquisition and development. Solitary monologues allow children to practise language and role-play situations where language is used. Make these cuddly personalized pillow puppets that can become special friends and companions.

What you need
- ✓ Plain white pillowcase
- ✓ Material for stuffing (cut up old fabric/ tights etc)
- ✓ Needle and thread, or sewing machine
- ✓ Glue
- ✓ Large felt shapes
- ✓ Pom poms

What you do

- Cut the pillowcase in half so that you have two square shapes.
- Sew all open ends, leaving a gap for stuffing.
- Stuff with old fabric or tights then sew the gap. Do not overstuff, the pillow puppets are best left slightly floppy
- Discuss eyes, noses and mouths with the children. What kind of shapes can they be?
- Provide the children with a pillow puppet each, felt shapes, pom poms and glue.
- Ask the children to make their own puppet face by gluing on the features.
- Write the children's names on the pillows.
- At the end of the session, collect the pillow puppets and sew the felt shapes securely.
- Sew a loop on the top of each puppet so it can be hung up. The puppets could live on the children's coat pegs.

The teddies' dressing room

This activity enables pairs of children to conduct a quiet conversation about dressing teddy bears. It encourages negotiation and decision making skills. Large teddy bears are ideal for dressing up, as they will fit in small children's clothes. Place the teddies and clothes in an enclosed play space to encourage quiet, focused conversation.

What you need

- ✓ A pop up play tent or den area
- ✓ Large teddy bears
- ✓ Selection of teddy size clothes and hats such as pants, vests, t shirts, jumpers, shorts, socks, mittens and hats
- ✓ Card, pen and string
- ✓ A dressing up box

What you do

- Place the teddies and dressing up clothes in the play space.
- Make a sign that reads: Teddies' Dressing Room and place by the play area.
- Invite two children into the dressing room to dress the bears for a 'teddy bears' day out'.

★ Teddies' ★
dressing room

Links

CLL LfC. 40+m

- Interact with others, negotiating plans and activities and taking turns in conversation.
- Play along side other children who are engaged in the same theme.

Shout it out!

Children love poetry. They find language patterns fun and will spontaneously create and play with rhyme, rhythm, assonance and alliteration so poetry is an ideal vehicle for developing language and literacy skills and for learning about our natural, physical, social, personal and numerical world. Children who have an understanding of rhyme and rhythm have an enriched understanding of language and feel confident and creative with literacy.

In this section you will find a variety of toy-themed rhymes, poems and activities. Each rhyme is accompanied by the following:

✓ Warm up activities to get mouths and bodies ready to rhyme!

✓ Tips on how to learn the rhyme together.

✓ Things to talk about relating to the rhyme that can be used in adult led discussion.

✓ Lists of words that may be new to all or some. These words can be explored for sound and meaning.

★ Enunciate clearly

When you recite a rhyme with children they look to your face for visual pronunciation cues. Over emphasize any tricky sounds. Be aware of the shapes your mouth is making.

★ Look around

Your face is very important – make sure everyone can see it. If the children are seated on the floor around you, make eye sweeps, turning your face from one side of the group to the other so every child gets a chance to see your face as you say the poem. Remember those closest to your feet may have the most restricted view.

Some general tips and suggestions

Why learn 'by heart'?

Rhymes are easy to memorize so information and vocabulary embedded in rhymes are remembered too. Learning to recite a short poem 'by heart' gives a child confidence. Reciting a short poem to adult friends, carers or family members gives a child a chance to perform, receive praise and feel comfortable speaking in front of others.

Some children love reciting rhymes in front of others while other children enjoy chanting rhymes as part of a group. Use your professional judgement and your knowledge of the children in your care to decide who might enjoy solo or group performances or who would perhaps feel more confident later in the year.

Remember to...

★ Move your body

Learning to recite rhymes is fun. Communicate your enthusiasm for rhyme and rhythm by moving your own body in time to the rhythm; clap your hands, stamp your feet, sway in time. Body movement is an important part of active learning.

Using toy rhymes

Children in your setting may know rhymes and songs with a toy theme that they have learnt at home.

Make a recording of toy-themed nursery rhymes

You could ask parents and carers if they can contribute toy rhymes of their own. Also ask your children if they know any toy rhymes in a language other than English. Make a recording of all the different versions and use it in your setting for listening activities.

Invite nursery rhyme 'listeners' to your setting

Invite parents and carers to visit your setting as 'listeners'. Explain to the visiting adults that their job is to listen to individual or groups of children recite rhymes and provide positive and appreciative feedback. If your setting is attached to or contained within a primary school, you could arrange for older children to help out as listeners.

If appropriate, you could put on a formal performance, but with younger children it is often better for the adult to move freely and informally around the setting to listen to individual or small groups of children. Make badges for your invited listeners so that the children can identify them as people who are ready to listen to their rhymes. You could make badges in the shape of an ear.

Popular toy nursery rhymes

Miss Polly had a dolly

Hobbyhorse

I had a little moppet

Teddy bear, teddy bear

Teddy bears' picnic.

I'm a little aeroplane

I'm a little aeroplane.
(stretch arms out to make wings)
See me in the sky.
I'll take you right around the world,
Flying really high.

I'm a little motorcar.
(place hands on steering wheel)
See my four round wheels.
I'll take us for a country drive.
So you can play in fields.

This activity enables children to:
- ✓ Focus on the long 'I' sound.
- ✓ Focus on the long 'e' sound.
- ✓ Discuss transport toys.
- ✓ Explore the idea of travel.

What you do

Warm up
- Practise being aeroplanes. Can you make an aeroplane sound?
- Practise being cars. Can you make a noise like a car?

Activity
- Recite the rhyme. Stress the words 'sky' and 'high' in the first verse and the words wheels and fields in the second verse.
- Ask the children to say the rhyme with you.

Talk about...

- ★ Aeroplanes. What do aeroplanes look like? Has anyone seen an aeroplane? Has anyone been in an aeroplane?
- ★ Cars. What do cars look like? Where can we go in the car? What do we put in a car to make it go?

Links

CLL LfC. 30-50m
- Join in with repeated refrains and anticipate key events and phrases in rhymes and stories.

CLL LfC. 40+m
- Listen with enjoyment and respond to stories, songs, music rhymes and poems and make up their own stories, songs rhymes and poems. (ELG)
- Extend their vocabulary, exploring the meanings and sounds of words. (ELG)

CD CM&D. 30-50m
- Sing a few familiar songs.
- Explore and learn how sounds can be changed.

Vocabulary

car   aeroplane   sky   wheels

Buckets and cups

Buckets and cups we all get wet.
Buckets and cups,
Buckets and cups,
Buckets and cups we all get wet.
We all get wet.

This activity enables children to:

✓ Practise the short 'u' sound.
✓ Talk about water play.
✓ Discuss containers.

What you do

Warm up

- Practise the short 'u' sound by opening your mouth wide and making short, sharp 'u' sounds.

Activity

- Recite the rhyme. Stress the short 'u' sound.
- Ask the children to recite the rhyme with you.

Talk about...

★ Buckets and cups. What can we put in a bucket?
★ What do we put in a cup?
★ Capacity. Which would hold more, a big bucket, or a little cup?

Links

CLL LfC. 30-50m

- Join in with repeated refrains and anticipate key events and phrases in rhymes and stories.

CLL LfC. 40+m

- Listen with enjoyment and respond to stories, songs, music rhymes and poems and make up their own stories, songs rhymes and poems. (ELG)
- Extend their vocabulary, exploring the meanings and sounds of words. (ELG)

CD CM&D. 30-50m

- Sing a few familiar songs.
- Explore and learn how sounds can be changed.

Vocabulary

bucket   cup   fill

Take turns

Take turns, take turns 1 2 3
Take turns, take turns
Come and play with me.
First we'll play your game
Then we'll play mine
We can play both games 3 4 5.

This activity enables children to:

✓ Understand the concept of turn taking.

✓ Practise numbers up to five.

✓ Explore rhyme.

✓ Practise the initial 't' sound.

Talk about..

★ Taking turns and sharing.

★ Why is it nice to share? Have you shared with anyone today? Who do you like to share with?

★ Why is it a good idea to take turns?

Links

CLL LfC. 30-50m

- Join in with repeated refrains and anticipate key events and phrases in rhymes and stories.

CLL LfC. 40+m

- Listen with enjoyment and respond to stories, songs, music rhymes and poems and make up their own stories, songs rhymes and poems. (ELG)
- Extend their vocabulary, exploring the meanings and sounds of words. (ELG)

CD CM&D. 30-50m

- Sing a few familiar songs.
- Explore and learn how sounds can be changed.

What you do

Warm up

- Practise making clear initial 't' sounds. Can you say, 'tip, top, tap'?
- Practise counting to five.

Activity

- Recite the rhyme, stressing the initial 't' sound.
- Ask the children to recite the rhyme with you.

Vocabulary

one   two   three   four   five

Shout it out!

Eat up dolly

Eat up dolly
Dib, dab, dib.
Messy dolly
Wear a bib!

Eat up dolly
Yum, yum, yum.
Happy dolly
Food is fun!

Talk about...

★ Eating. Why do we wash our hands before we eat?

★ Everybody spills things. What we do if we accidentally spill something. Remind the children that people are always happy to help them.

★ What is your favourite food?

★ What food is fun to eat?

This activity enables children to:

✓ Practise the short 'o' sound.

✓ Practise the short 'I' sound.

✓ Practise the short 'u' sound.

✓ Discuss eating.

pop!

pip

What you do

Warm up

● Make three short 'o' sounds.

● Can you say 'pop pop pop'?

● Make three short 'i' sounds.

● Can you say, 'pip pip pip'?

● Make three short 'u' sounds.

● Can you say 'pup pup pup'?

Activity

● Recite the rhyme, stressing the middle 'o', 'i' and 'u' sounds.

● Recite with the children.

Links

CLL LfC. 30-50m

· Join in with repeated refrains and anticipate key events and phrases in rhymes and stories.

CLL LfC. 40+m

· Listen with enjoyment and respond to stories, songs, music rhymes and poems and make up their own stories, songs rhymes and poems. (ELG)

· Extend their vocabulary, exploring the meanings and sounds of words. (ELG)

CD CM&D. 30-50m

· Sing a few familiar songs.

· Explore and learn how sounds can be changed.

Vocabulary

eat   bib   happy   food

Bang the drum

Boom boom!
(bang drum, or clap hands)
Bang my drum.
Boom boom!
(bang drum, or clap hands)
With my thumb.

Boom boom!
(bang drum, or clap hands)
It's lots of fun.
Boom boom!
(bang drum, or clap hands)
Bang my drum.

Talk about...

★ Things that make good drums.

★ Things that make a good noise when we hit them with a pencil. Do different objects make different sounds?

★ What is your favourite sound?

This activity enables children to:

✓ Practise the initial 'b' sound.

✓ Practise the 'oo' sound.

✓ Practise the short 'u' sound.

✓ Make lots of noise!

What you do

Warm up

• Practise saying, 'boom boom!' Can you say it very loudly?

• Enjoy making the initial 'b' sound and the final 'm' sound. Feel your lips moving apart and coming together.

Activity

• Give the children a drum, tub or box to bang. If none are available, you can clap your hands.

• Recite the rhyme to the children.

• Recite with the children making lots of bangs and noise!

Links

CLL LfC. 30-50m

• Join in with repeated refrains and anticipate key events and phrases in rhymes and stories.

CLL LfC. 40+m

• Listen with enjoyment and respond to stories, songs, music rhymes and poems and make up their own stories, songs rhymes and poems. (ELG)

• Extend their vocabulary, exploring the meanings and sounds of words. (ELG)

CD CM&D. 30-50m

• Sing a few familiar songs.

• Explore and learn how sounds can be changed.

Vocabulary

bang   drum   thumb

Cuddle bear

Cuddle bear, Cuddle bear,
Snuggle bear, Snuggle bear,
Huddle him up. Put on a hat.

Cuddle bear, Cuddle bear,
Snuggle bear, Snuggle bear,
Wrap him all up. Give him a pat.

This activity enables children to:

✓ Practise the short 'u' sound.

✓ Discuss how to care for something or someone.

✓ Explore rhyme.

What you do

Warm up

- Practise the short 'u' sound by finding words that rhyme with cuddle. These can be silly words!

  cuddle snuggle

  wuddle huddle

  fuddle buggle

Activity

- Recite the rhyme.

- Recite the rhyme with the children.

- Give the children a soft toy each and encourage them to bounce the toys on their lap as they recite the rhyme.

cuddle

wuddle

Links

CLL LfC. 30-50m

- Join in with repeated refrains and anticipate key events and phrases in rhymes and stories.

CLL LfC. 40+m

- Listen with enjoyment and respond to stories, songs, music rhymes and poems and make up their own stories, songs rhymes and poems. (ELG)

- Extend their vocabulary, exploring the meanings and sounds of words. (ELG)

CD CM&D. 30-50m

- Sing a few familiar songs.

- Explore and learn how sounds can be changed.

Vocabulary

cuddle snuggle huddle

Building tall

*Building, building,
building tall*

*Up, up, up we build our
wall*
(move arms up)

*Building, building,
building tall*

*Down, down, down
you're going to fall!*
(shake arms down)

Talk about...

★ Things that are made
with brick walls. There
are walls all around us.
Houses, and shops have
walls. There are walls
around gardens and
parks.

★ Walls can be made from
different types of bricks
and stones. Can you
spot any when you are
out and about?

**This activity enables
children to:**

✓ Explore rhyme

✓ Discuss construction
activities

What you do

Warm up

- Practise moving your arms
up and stretching tall while
saying, 'up up up!'

- Practise shaking down to
the ground while saying,
'down, down down!'

Activity

- Recite the rhyme to the
children.

- Recite the rhyme with
the children joining in the
actions.

Links

CLL LfC. 30-50m

- Join in with repeated refrains and
anticipate key events and phrases in
rhymes and stories.

CLL LfC. 40+m

- Listen with enjoyment and respond
to stories, songs, music rhymes and
poems and make up their own stories,
songs rhymes and poems. (ELG)

- Extend their vocabulary, exploring the
meanings and sounds of words. (ELG)

CD CM&D. 30-50m

- Sing a few familiar songs.

- Explore and learn how sounds can be
changed.

Vocabulary

building   wall   up   down

Ride around

Cars go   Buses go
Beep beep   *Beep beep*
Beep beep   *Beep beep*
(press horn)   *(press horn)*
Smelly feet!   *Welly feet!*

Vans go   *Smelly, jelly,*
Beep beep   *welly feet!*
Beep beep
(press horn)
Jelly feet!

This activity enables children to:

✓ Explore rhyme.

✓ Discuss transport.

✓ Practise the long 'e' sound.

Talk about...

★ Transport. What do we travel in? What is your favourite form of transport?

★ Do you have toys you can ride on? Do they have horns or bells?

What you do

Warm up

- Make long, loud 'beeps'.

- Enjoy making the initial 'b' and final 'p' sound. Feel your lips move apart then come together.

Activity

- Recite the rhyme to the children.

- Recite the rhyme with the children, making plenty of loud beeps!

Links

CLL LfC. 30-50m

· Join in with repeated refrains and anticipate key events and phrases in rhymes and stories.

CLL LfC. 40+m

· Listen with enjoyment and respond to stories, songs, music rhymes and poems and make up their own stories, songs rhymes and poems. (ELG)

· Extend their vocabulary, exploring the meanings and sounds of words. (ELG)

CD CM&D. 30-50m

· Sing a few familiar songs.

· Explore and learn how sounds can be changed.

Vocabulary

car   bus   van

Doctor, doctor

Doctor, Doctor, I'm feeling ill.
Give me some medicine.
Give me a pill.
Bandage my leg.
Stick on a plaster.
Make me get better not slower
but faster.

I'll be your doctor.
I'll be your nurse.
I'll make you feel better,
And not ten times worse.

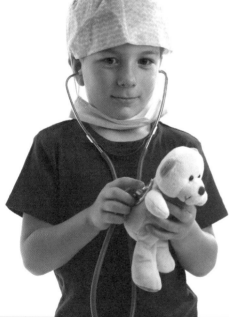

This activity enables children to:
- ✓ Discuss feeling poorly.
- ✓ Explore rhyme.
- ✓ Discuss visiting the doctor or nurse.

What you do

Warm up

- Explore medical equipment. Look at bandages, plasters and thermometers

Activity

- Recite the rhyme.
- Recite the rhyme with the children.

Talk about...

- ★ What doctors and nurses do to make us well. Have you ever been to hospital? In hospital doctors and nurses are very kind and will make you feel better again.
- ★ If you feel poorly at home what do you do to feel better?

Links

CLL LfC. 30-50m

- Join in with repeated refrains and anticipate key events and phrases in rhymes and stories.

CLL LfC. 40+m

- Listen with enjoyment and respond to stories, songs, music rhymes and poems and make up their own stories, songs rhymes and poems. (ELG)
- Extend their vocabulary, exploring the meanings and sounds of words. (ELG)

CD CM&D. 30-50m

- Sing a few familiar songs.
- Explore and learn how sounds can be changed.

Vocabulary

doctor   nurse   medicine   plaster

Shout it out!

Tongue tricks

Reciting tongue twisters is an excellent way of learning to pronounce letter sounds and combinations clearly. It is enormous fun for children and practitioners alike. The fact that adults find tongue twisters just as tricky as children is often a source of amusement and creates a positive environment for learning literacy skills.

In this section you will find a variety of toy-themed tongue twisters. Each is accompanied by warm up exercises for the mouth that are both silly and fun but very important to tongue twisting success!

✓ The exercises focus on what we do with our teeth, tongue and lips to produce a sound or a series of sounds.

✓ The formation of each letter sound is summed up by a sentence that can be used as a mnemonic device (a way of remembering).

✓ The exercises lead up to a short tongue twister challenge, which, while achievable for adult and child alike, is still tricky enough to trip you up and induce a serious fit of the giggles!

Tongue twisters are difficult. The activities in this chapter are not designed to be achieved perfectly but rather are created for language fun. Playing with tongue twisters involves the acknowledgement of failure and the often hilarious struggle to master something that is very difficult. By striving to pronounce clearly alongside an adult, who is participating in the game as an equal, children can grow in confidence (and competitiveness!).

Remember

Children learn to produce speech sounds at different rates. Be positive and encouraging as attempts to articulate initial letters and blends are made. You are not making mistakes: you are having fun!

Pink kite

The 'k' and 'p' sounds

The 'k' sound is made by lifting the back of the tongue to the roof of the mouth. Air builds up behind the tongue and makes an exploding sound as the mouth is opened. The 'k' sound makes your breath kick!

The 'p' sound is made by pressing the lips together. Air is built up behind them and then as the mouth opens an exploding sound is made.
The 'p' makes your breath pop!

Practise making 'k's and 'p's

- Hold your hand up in front of your mouth as you make the 'k' sound. Can you feel your breath on your hand as you make a quick, sharp 'k' kick sound?
- Make five 'k' kicks with your breath on your hand.
- Hold your hand in front of your mouth as you make the 'p' sound.
- Can you feel your breath as you make a quick sharp popping 'p' sound?
- Make five quick sharp 'p' pops with your breath on your hand.

Say: kick, kick, kick

Say: could you cuddle a cat?
         could you cuddle a cloud?

Say: pick, pick, pick

Say: pigs pick pears
         pigs pick potatoes

Now your mouth has warmed up with all those 'p's and 'k's you are ready for the tongue twister.

Links

CD CM&D. 30-50m.
- Explore and learn how sounds can be changed.

CLL LfC. 40+m
- Enjoy listening to and using spoken and written language, and readily use it in their play and learning. (ELG)

CLL LS&L. 30-50m
- Show awareness of rhyme and alliteration.

CLL LS&L. 40+m
- Hear and say the initial sound in words and know which letters represent some of the sounds.
- Hear and say sounds in words in the order in which they occur. (ELG)

Pink kite

Pink kite
Purple kite
I pick a pretty kite.

Blue paintbrush

The 'p' and 'b' sounds

The 'p' sound is made by pressing the lips together. Air is built up behind them and then as the mouth opens an exploding sound is made.
The 'p' sound makes your breath pop!

The 'b' sound is made by pressing the lips together and then gently letting your breath bubble through them.
The 'b' sound blows beautiful bubbles!

Practise making 'p's and 'b's

- Hold your hand in front of your mouth as you make the 'p' sound. Can you feel your breath as you make a quick sharp popping 'p' sound?

- Make four quick sharp 'p' pops with your breath on your hand.

- Hold your hand in front of your mouth as you make the 'b' sound. Can you feel your breath as you make beautiful 'b' sounds?

- Make four bubble 'bs' on your hand

Say: pick, pick, pick

Say: pick up puppets

Say: bob, bob, bob

Say: bob, big, bubbles.

Now your mouth has warmed up with all those 'p's and 'b's you are ready for the tongue twister.

Links

CD CM&D. 30-50m.
- Explore and learn how sounds can be changed.

CLL LfC. 40+m
- Enjoy listening to and using spoken and written language, and readily use it in their play. (ELG)

CLL LS&L. 30-50m
- Show awareness of rhyme and alliteration.

CLL LS&L. 40+m
- Hear and say the initial sound in words and know which letters represent some of the sounds.
- Hear and say sounds in words in the order in which they occur. (ELG)

Blue paintbrush

Blue paintbrush
Black paintbrush
Blob, blob, blob

New mops

The 'm' and 'n' sounds

The 'm' sound is made by pressing your lips together and humming.
The 'm' sound hums.
mmmm mmmm mmmm

The 'n' sound is made by opening the mouth slightly, placing the tip of the tongue towards the front of the roof of the mouth and then bringing it down sharply.
The 'n' sound is nice not nasty!

Practise making 'm's and 'n's

- Press your lips together tightly and make a long 'mmmm' sound.
- Open your lips sharply after a count of three.
- Make four quick 'n' sounds.

Links

CD CM&D. 30-50m.
- Explore and learn how sounds can be changed.

CLL LfC. 40+m
- Enjoy listening to and using spoken and written language, and readily use it in their play. (ELG)

CLL LS&L. 30-50m
- Show awareness of rhyme and alliteration.

CLL LS&L. 40+m
- Hear and say the initial sound in words and know which letters represent some of the sounds.
- Hear and say sounds in words in the order in which they occur. (ELG)

Say: mum, mum, mum

Say: mum makes muffins

Say: no, no, no

Say: no new nets.

Now your mouth has warmed up with all those 'm's and 'n's you are ready for the tongue twister.

New mop

New mop
My nice new mop
Mops nicely

Sally doll is sleeping

The 's' and 'sh' sounds

The 's' sound is made by putting the teeth together and hissing air out between them. The 's' sound makes you hiss!
Hiss, hiss, hiss, hiss

The 'sh' sound is made by opening your mouth and pushing the lips forward slightly, the teeth are then pushed together and air pushed through.
The 'sh' sound pushes and whooshes.

Practise making 's's and 'sh's

- Open your mouth, put your teeth together and hiss like a snake.
- Make four long hissing 's' sounds.
- Place you hand in front of your mouth and make four long hard 'sh' sounds.

> Say: sun, sun, sun
>
> Say: sun, sea, sand
>
> Say: shell, shell, shell
>
> Say: shells shiver

Links

CD CM&D. 30-50m.
- Explore and learn how sounds can be changed.

CLL LfC. 40+m
- Enjoy listening to and using spoken and written language, and readily use it in their play. (ELG)

CLL LS&L. 30-50m
- Show awareness of rhyme and alliteration.

CLL LS&L. 40+m
- Hear and say the initial sound in words and know which letters represent some of the sounds.
- Hear and say sounds in words in the order in which they occur. (ELG)

Now your mouth has warmed up with all those 's's and 'sh's you are ready for the tongue twister.

Sally doll is sleeping

Sally doll is sleeping, Sh!

Sally doll is snoring, Sh!

Sh, Sally doll!

ssshhhh!

Vroom fast

The 'f' and 'v' sounds

The 'f' sound is made by placing your top teeth lightly in the middle of your lower lip and blowing.
The 'f' sound feels funny!

The 'v' sound is made by placing your top teeth firmly in the middle of your lower lip.
The 'v' sound is very vain.

Practise making 'f's and 'v's

- Can you make four funny 'f' sounds?
- Can you make four vain 'v' sounds?

Links

CD CM&D. 30-50m.
- Explore and learn how sounds can be changed.

CLL LfC. 40+m
- Enjoy listening to and using spoken and written language, and readily use it in their play. (ELG)

CLL LS&L. 30-50m
- Show awareness of rhyme and alliteration.

CLL LS&L. 40+m
- Hear and say the initial sound in words and know which letters represent some of the sounds.
- Hear and say sounds in words in the order in which they occur. (ELG)

Say: f

Say: fee fi fo fum

Say: v

Say: violet violin

Now your mouth has warmed up with all those 'f's and 'v's you are ready for the tongue twister.

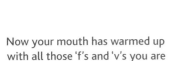

Vroom fast

Vroom fast van
Vroom very fast.
Vroom van vroom
Vroom very, very fast!

Dotty teddy

The 'd' and 't' sounds

The 'd' sound is made by quickly touching the tip of the tongue to the roof of the mouth, just behind the teeth, and then dipping it back.

The 'd' sound dips and dives.

Place your hand lightly under your chin and make four dipping 'd' sounds

The 't' sound is made by putting your teeth together and then opening them.

The 't' sound makes your teeth tingle.

Place your hand in front of your mouth and make four 't' sounds. Feel your breath on your hand.

Practise making 'd's and 't's

- Can you make four dipping 'd' sounds?
- Can you make four tingling 't' sounds?

Now your mouth has warmed up with all those 'ds' and 'ts' you are ready for the tongue twister.

Say: do, do, do

Say: do, don't, do, don't

Say: tap, tap, tap

Say: tip, tap, tip, tap

Dotty teddy

Dotty teddy
Teddy dot.
Dotty teddy
Teddy dot.

Links

CD CM&D. 30-50m.
- Explore and learn how sounds can be changed.

CLL LfC. 40+m
- Enjoy listening to and using spoken and written language, and readily use it in their play. (ELG)

CLL LS&L. 30-50m
- Show awareness of rhyme and alliteration.

CLL LS&L. 40+m
- Hear and say the initial sound in words and know which letters represent some of the sounds.
- Hear and say sounds in words in the order in which they occur. (ELG)

Wiggle rabbit

The 'r' and 'w' sounds

The 'r' sound is made by resting your top teeth just inside your bottom lip and then ripping them apart quickly.
The 'r' sound rests then rips!

The 'w' sound is made forming the lips into a tight circle, then opening them.
The 'w' sound wishes you well.

Practise making 'r's and 'w's

- Can you make four ripping 'r' sounds?
- Can you make four wishing 'w' sounds?

Say: run, run, run

Say: run, rabbit, run

Say: well, well, well

Say: wellies win, wellies win

Links

CD CM&D. 30-50m.

- Explore and learn how sounds can be changed.

CLL LfC. 40+m

- Enjoy listening to and using spoken and written language, and readily use it in their play. (ELG)

CLL LS&L. 30-50m

- Show awareness of rhyme and alliteration.

CLL LS&L. 40+m

- Hear and say the initial sound in words and know which letters represent some of the sounds.
- Hear and say sounds in words in the order in which they occur. (ELG)

Now your mouth has warmed up with all those 'r's and 'w's you are ready for the tongue twister.

Wiggle rabbit

Wiggle rabbit

Woo woo

Wiggle rabbit

Woo

Let's tell stories!

The activities in this section encourage children to join in with the telling of a story. By allowing children to offer their own ideas and take the story in new directions the practitioner and the child engage in creative language play together. The practitioner offers a framework to support the child's ideas and encourages creative language development by reinforcing, extending, modelling and naming vocabulary.

Listening to stories helps children to:

✓ extend their vocabulary.

✓ experience a variety of linguistic constructions.

✓ enjoy creative language.

✓ have fun!

Telling stories helps children to:

✓ organize their thoughts.

✓ extend their vocabulary.

✓ learn to capture and hold the interest of the listener.

✓ sequence events.

✓ have fun!

Dialogic reading

What is dialogic reading?

Everyone loves stories. We love to listen to stories and we love to tell stories. Dialogic reading is where listening and telling are combined. It describes a learning situation where adult and child, or child and child, have a conversation about the story. Dialogic reading is based initially around three points.

1. Asking 'what' and 'where' questions

For example:

Adult: "What do you think the dinosaur is going to do next?"

Child: "He's going to eat the trees."

Adult: "Where will he go then?"

Child: "He'll go in the river."

2. Asking open-ended questions

Avoid 'yes' 'no' answers. Open-ended questions often start with 'why'. Open-ended questions don't prompt a particular answer but are invitations to express an opinion or to encourage further discussion.

For example:

Adult: "Why do you think the rabbit is sad?"

Child: "He's sad because his friend has gone home."

Adult: "Really? Why does that make him sad?"

Child: "I think he wants to play longer."

3. Repeat and expand

A child's response is always valuable. Make sure they know this by repeating what they have said in whole or in part and using this opportunity to model correct grammar and pronunciation.

The introduction of new vocabulary is particularly effective in a dialogic reading situation. A new word can be introduced in context, in a focused situation and often with a picture to illustrate the word. Try to keep expanded phrases short to encourage repetition.

For example:

Child: "I tink dat dog is cared"

Adult: "Oh, really? You think that the dog is scared? Why do you think he is scared? Is he scared of the enormous cat?"

With very young children, the adult can take on both roles in the dialogue, modelling both question and answers.

Dialogic reading and picture books

Picture books provide a perfect opportunity for exploring a story together. Use picture books to encourage your children to:

- explore character's emotions. How does the character feel? What makes you think that?
- describe a situation in their own words.
- predict what is going to happen.

Dialogic reading without pictures

Picture books are a large part of story sharing in the early years. However, it is also important to tell stories without pictures.

By telling stories with words alone you are:

- allowing children to create their own images of the story.
- encouraging attentive listening.
- modelling oral story telling to the children.

Remember: Dialogic reading is shared reading, and sharing is above all about warmth and enjoyment. The most important thing you can do is to share your love of stories.

Some suggestions for stories suitable for dialogic reading

Where's my Teddy?
by Jez Alborough (Walker Books)

Toyland stories series
by Enid Blyton (Harper Collins)

Peace at last
by Jill Murphy (Campbell Books)

Being a story teller

When telling a story:

- ✓ practise telling the story beforehand.
- ✓ be expressive – use your face and body to make the story come alive.
- ✓ use different voices to differentiate between characters.
- ✓ be dramatic – use pauses to heighten tension.
- ✓ look around the group as you tell the story. Use eye-sweeps to include every child.
- ✓ make eye contact with those who are finding it difficult to settle or whose attention may be wandering.

When reading from a book:

- ✓ if the story is new to you, look at it beforehand.
- ✓ decide on character voices beforehand (and be consistent!).
- ✓ if you there are no pictures to share, lay the book on your lap. Raise your head and speak to the group, dipping your eyes to read the next lines.

Sharing picture books with a group

There are certain practical difficulties in sharing a picture book with a group of children. Unless you are using a big book with a support frame it can be physically awkward to keep turning the book between yourself and the children. All too often, children at the periphery of the group spend too much time twisting, turning and fidgeting in order to see what is going on. If a child cannot see clearly they may become disengaged with the story.

Remember to:

- familiarize yourself with the book beforehand. Make sure you know what is happening in each picture.
- have a clear idea in your mind of the kinds of questions you are going to ask and the areas you are going to explore, but also be ready to take the talk in unexpected directions.
- turn the book slowly at every stage so all children have a clear view.
- check children's faces to ensure all are engaged with the book.
- pay attention to those who may be losing focus. Try asking an open question to re-engage wandering minds.

Toy story templates

These toy-themed story templates allow practitioners to create guided storytelling play. By offering a story structure practitioners can help children to:

- think logically and place events in sequence.
- imagine consequences to actions.
- model and expand vocabulary.
- feel a sense of ownership over a story.

Guided storytelling means that practitioner and child work together to create a story. It is important that you are flexible, allowing the children to make imaginative contributions no matter how unlikely the scenario becomes! However, it is important to remember your role as an educator as well as a facilitator.

Remember to:

- repeat a word or phrase, modeling the correct pronunciation.
- repeat a word or phrase that is an example of good language use.
- give praise to a reluctant or nervous contributor.
- follow up a child's suggestion with a further 'what' question.

'What' prompts

Use 'what' prompts to encourage creative thinking and extend vocabulary:

What colour was it?

What did it look like?

What did she do next?

What was he wearing?

What you do

- ✓ Gather your group of children and seat them.
- ✓ Tell the story, pausing and asking for suggestions where indicated.
- ✓ If the children are reluctant to contribute, draw suggestions on a whiteboard or on paper. Don't worry, your drawings don't have to be accurate; they are prompts that help stimulate discussion. If you tried to draw an ambulance and a child shouts out "it's a fire engine", say: "that's brilliant; you think they arrived on a fire engine. What colour is it do you think?"

Remember to:

- show respect and enthusiasm for all suggestions.
- repeat each child's suggestion clearly, extending and developing vocabulary and grammar if necessary. Repeat once, while looking directly at the child and then again to the whole group.
- speak clearly, varying your tone and pitch to make the story exciting and engaging.

Story template 1:
The bear that loved honey

Once upon a time there was a teddy bear that loved honey. He loved honey very much. He had honey for breakfast, honey for lunch and honey for tea.

What colour was teddy bear?

One day he looked in his cupboard for some honey, but there wasn't any there. He looked around the kitchen.

Where else in the kitchen might he find a jar of honey?

There was no honey to be found. The bear decided to go and ask the bees.

Where do you think the bees lived?

He went into the garden and walked towards the beehive. Suddenly he tripped and fell over.

What did he fall into?

The bees felt sorry for teddy. They showed him where there was lots of honey. Teddy collected the honey and took it back to his house.

And what do you think he had for his tea?

Links *for all story templates*

CLL LfC. 30-50m
- Listen to stories with increasing attention and recall.
- Describe main story settings, vents and principal characters.

CLL Reading. 30-50m
- Begin to be aware of the ways stories are structured.
- Suggest how the story might end.

Story template 2:
The bouncy ball

Once upon a time there was a ball that just couldn't stop bouncing. Bounce, bounce, bounce.

What colour was the ball?

His favourite place to bounce was against the wall in the playground. One day the little boy who was playing with him bounced him too hard and he flew over the wall.

Where did he land?

He started to roll, faster and faster until he landed at a pair of feet.

Who's feet were they?

What did they do with the ball?

The ball wanted to be back in the playground, so he bounced and he bounced and he bounced right back up the hill.

Someone was walking past.

Who was it?

They said, "look at that beautiful bouncy ball. That belongs in the playground. I'd better throw it back."

So they did. The bouncy ball was pleased to be home again.

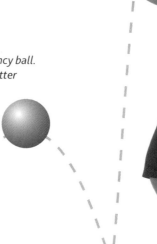

Story template 3:
The magic bricks

John had a box of magic bricks. The bricks could turn into anything that John decided to build. If he built a castle then, whoosh! A castle would appear. If he built a racing car then, zoom! A racing car would be there. John opened his box of bricks. "I wonder what I should build today?" he said.

What should John build?

What did it look like?

What did John do next?

John was very tired; he closed his eyes and wished the bricks back in the box. There was a 'pop, pop, pop' sound, and when he opened his eyes the bricks were back in the box. John was hungry after his adventure. So home he went for tea.

Story sequencing

The ability to organise a story into a beginning, a middle and an end can be difficult for young children. You may find that children remember the most exciting part of a story or focus on a particular aspect that appeals to them. By practising story sequencing skills children learn to:

- organise their thoughts clearly.
- attend to narrative.
- improve their ability to comprehend.
- understand the concept of consequences.
- recollect facts and incidents.
- articulate their thoughts clearly.
- manage practical tasks.

The following suggestions are for practical toy-themed sequencing activities and include making story cards, picture books and story sacks.

Sequencing cards

Make sequencing cards for your favourite toy-themed stories. You don't have to be good at drawing – be resourceful! Find relevant pictures in magazines or on the internet.

What you need

- ✓ A toy-themed story
- ✓ Thick card
- ✓ Pens /pencils/ found images
- ✓ Glue
- ✓ Scissors

What you do

- Choose a story with a simple plot. Break the narrative into sections and decide on the images that go with each point in the plot.
- If you have broken down your story into six main points, cut out six squares of card (approx 8cm x 8cm).
- Draw/paste images of each of the plot points on the cards.
- Laminate the cards if you can.
- Tell the story to the children.
- Discuss the main points or events in the story.
- Engage the group in a retelling of the story.
- Introduce the sequencing cards – discuss the images in each one.
- Ask an individual or group of children if they can place the cards in order.
- Talk through the order that they've chosen. Is it correct? Do you all agree?

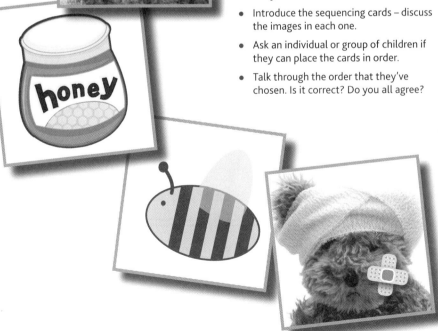

Doll's day out sequencing cards

It's not only fictional stories that can be sequenced. Instructional activities provide excellent material for creating sequencing activities. Talk about dressing toys for a day out in the park, or how you would make a sandcastle in a sand pit.

What you need
- ✓ Card
- ✓ Felt tip pens
- ✓ Scissors

What you do

- Talk about what you would need to do to get a doll dressed for a day out.

  You could:

  1. Put on dress
  2. Put on shoes
  3. Do up straps or laces
  4. Put on coat
  5. Do up buttons or zip
  6. Put on hat

- Cut six squares of card (8cm x 8cm).
- Draw each stage of preparing the doll for the park on separate cards.
- Laminate each card if possible.
- Ask the children to sequence the cards.
- Discuss their choices. Do you all agree?

Building a sandcastle sequencing cards

What you need
- ✓ Card
- ✓ Felt tip pens
- ✓ Scissors

What you do
- Cut five squares of card (8cm x 8cm).
- Draw each stage of making a sandcastle on the card.

You could:

1. Collect bucket and spade
2. Scoop sand in the bucket
3. Turn the bucket over carefully and pat it
4. Lift the bucket
5. Place a flag in the top

- Laminate the cards if possible.
- Ask the children to sequence the cards.
- Discuss their choices. Do you all agree?

Links *for sequencing activities*

CLL LfT. 40+m
- Begin to make patterns in their experience through linking cause and effect, sequencing, ordering and grouping.
- Begin to use talk instead of action to rehearse, reorder and reflect on past experience, linking significant events from own experience and from stories, paying attention to how events lead into one another.

CLL Reading. 40+m
- Retell narratives in the correct sequence drawing on language patterns of stories. (ELG)

KUW Time. 30-50m
- Talk about past and future events.

Make your own 'Toy Story' picture book

Make your own book about toys and their adventures. Display it where everyone can see it. Give it to each child in turn to take home to show parents and carers, and make it easily available for language play in and around your setting.

Making your own book enables children to:

- Understand how books are created.
- Talk about what they have seen.
- Make decisions and organise their thoughts.
- Put events into sequence.
- Place objects in categories.

What you need
- ✓ Card
- ✓ Hole punch
- ✓ Treasury tags
- ✓ Toy pictures

What you do

- There are many different types of toy books to make. You could make:
  - A book about different toys in your setting. You could have different chapters for different types of toys.
  - A book with a page for each child in your setting, displaying photos and child drawn pictures of their favourite toy. Interview the children about the toys and add this as text.
- Arrange for a toy to have a holiday (with a practitioner). Take photos of the toy in various locations. Place the photos in a book with some explanatory text. The toy could perhaps go shopping on a Saturday, or spend the day at the beach.

Links

CLL Reading. 30-50m
- Know information can be relayed in the form of print.
- Show interest in illustrations and print in books and print in the environment.

CLL Reading. 40+m
- Know that information can be retrieved from books and computers.

Talk about...

Initiate a discussion about what kind of book or books you could make. Remember, when leading discussions with the very young, it's important to respond to and appreciate all contributions. Repeat suggestions to the whole group, modeling correct grammar and pronunciation.

Toy Story

Make your own toy story sacks

Story sacks are very popular in early years settings. They are available commercially but are fun to put together yourself. Story sacks usually contain a book and items and characters relevant to the story. In this activity, however, the book is missing. Instead, children take out a series of toy-themed objects in turn and create a story around them.

What you do

- Seat the children.
- Say, "Once upon a time there was a…"
- Choose a child to take two items out of the sack.
- Ask for story suggestions about the two items.
- Continue taking one or two items out at a time asking the question, "What happened next?"
- Suggest story ideas yourself until children become confident with their own suggestions.
- When the last items have been withdrawn ask for endings to the story.

What you need

- ✓ A sack or draw string bag
- ✓ Toys and objects (at least 10). These can be toys or items from small world play or even pictures and photographs.

Links

CLL LfT. 30-50m

- Use talk to connect ideas explain what is happening and anticipate what might happen next.

CLL LfC. 30-50m

- Describe main story settings, events and principal characters.
- Use a widening range of words to express or elaborate on ideas.

Let's pretend!

Children learn and develop language in a social context. This means that language learning is active learning – children 'do' talk. Playing pretend or role-play allows children to 'do' talk while exploring a situation they are in control of and feel comfortable with.

Role-play

Role-play is an important way for young children to develop and practise language skills. By participating in role-play children:

- ✓ Learn subject specific vocabulary.
- ✓ Learn the importance of talk in a given situation.
- ✓ Use observational and recall skills to remember and reproduce a situation or series of actions.
- ✓ Understand the feelings and needs of others.
- ✓ Listen to others and follow up on what has been said.

Remember...

Don't worry too much about having the right role-play equipment. Children often explore complex and creative role-playing scenarios with no physical prompts or props at all. Sometimes all that is needed to inspire role-play is exposure to the initial role itself.

The dressing up box and toys

A well stocked dressing up box is a must for any early years setting. Dressing up games allow children to inhabit the role they are playing and often prompts new and complex language use.

A large dressing up box, containing a jumble of clothes and props, provides children with plenty of opportunity for talk. As items are sorted through, accepted or rejected, play is negotiated and created. If there is a jumble of ideas to navigate, all sorts of play possibilities can emerge. A jumble box can contain all sorts of things. Children often find role play possibilities in the most unlikely of items.

Introducing toys to dressing up games encourages new play directions and inspires imaginative language. Include toys in dressing up games by placing them in the dressing up box. The toys will emerge as the clothes are explored, the toys are then incorporated into the play.

Try placing some of these toys in your dressing up box:

- Soft animal toys
- A baby doll
- Teddy bears
- Character puppets

New, complex language emerges when children attempt to describe and negotiate new situations and play new scenarios. Stimulate language by offering the children new and unexpected toy items. Change the items regularly.

Try placing some of these items in your dressing up box:

- A toy kettle
- A toy phone
- A treasure chest
- A toy hammer

Use your imagination. Keep a look out for interesting and unusual toys that could be incorporated into your children's dressing up play.

Topic specific boxes

If you are exploring a particular topic and want to reinforce topic vocabulary it may be useful to present the children with clothes, toys and props that are grouped. As you set out the box, provide a springboard for play by talking about the topic. See the suggestions on the following pages (51-52).

Links *for all role-play activities*

CD DI&IP. 30-50m

- Engage in imaginative play and role-play based on own firsthand experience.
- Notice what adults do, imitating what is observed and then doing it spontaneously when the adult is not there.

KUW Place. 30-50m.

- Show an interest in the world in which they live.

Let's pretend!

Doctors and nurses box

Talk about...

★ What bandages and plasters are for.

★ Where doctors and nurses work.

★ What kind of injuries you might find in a hospital.

★ Why we take medicine (stress that only adults give real medicine).

★ Where our heart is. Can you hear it beating?

What you need

✓ Bandages

✓ Stickers for plasters

✓ Toy stethoscope

✓ Spoons for medicine

✓ Prescription pad and pencil

✓ Injured toys

✓ Small blankets

✓ White aprons and hats

✓ Doctor's coat/ small white shirt.

Gardener's box

What you need

✓ Plastic plant pots

✓ Overalls

✓ Caps

✓ Buckets and spades

✓ Artificial flowers and plants

✓ Watering cans

Talk about...

★ What plants need to make them grow.

★ What we wear to protect our clothes when we are gardening.

★ What are our favourite plants.

★ What kind of plants are good to eat.

Princes and princesses box

What you need

- ✓ Cloaks
- ✓ Velvet and satin fabric to make cloak
- ✓ Crowns
- ✓ Tiaras
- ✓ Jewels
- ✓ Bangles and bracelets
- ✓ Treasure chests
- ✓ Pretend coins

Talk about...

- ★ Jewels, gold and silver.
- ★ Do you know the names of some gems? A diamond is white, a ruby is red, a sapphire is blue and an emerald is green.

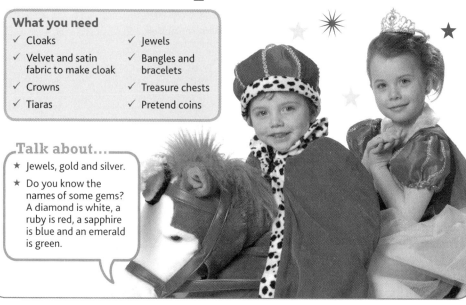

Animals box

Talk about...

- ★ What are your favourite animals?
- ★ Do you have any pets?
- ★ What sounds do these animals make?

  Cows   Pigs   Sheep,
  Horses   Mice   Ducks

- ★ Can you make more animal noises?

What you need

- ✓ Animal toys
- ✓ Soft toys
- ✓ Model animals
- ✓ Animal costumes.

Make a variety of animal tails.

What you do

- Make a belt from any fabric by cutting a strip and sewing velcro on each end.
- Cut a strip of fur fabric and stitch it to the back of the belt to make a tail.

Make a variety of animal ears.

What you do

- Make a head band from a strip of fabric, sewing velcro on each end.
- Make ears from off cuts of fur fabric and attach them to the band.

Let's pretend!

Role-play areas with toys

Permanent or semi permanent role-play areas provide children with plenty of opportunities for talk. However, it has been shown that children's language develops when new situations are introduced to the role-play. Try suggesting these role-play interventions to stretch language use. Each intervention introduces a new toy and a new event to the play.

In the house

The house is a favourite place to play. Children role-play everyday lives and explore common events such as meal times, washing up, bath time and bed time.

Interventions.

- Someone is coming to tea.
- A guest is going to stay for the night.
- You are preparing for a party.

What you do

- Provide the children with the role-play area.
- Observe the play. Use your professional judgement to decide when to introduce a new toy and play suggestion (intervention).
- Enter the play, introducing the toy who is coming to tea, or the toy who will be an overnight house guest.
- Withdraw from the play.

What you need

- ✓ Home corner/ house
- ✓ Kitchen equipment: cooker, dishes, cutlery, ironing board etc
- ✓ Bedroom furniture: cot, bed, bedding.
- ✓ Human or animal toys

At the garage

Garages can be set up to service ride-on toys and small cars and trucks. Provide a box and hose for a petrol pump, and a till to take payment. Many garages are also shops. Have some food items available for hungry drivers. Provide tools for your young mechanics.

Interventions.

- A race is coming through town and all the cars need petrol.
- Two cars bump and need fixing.
- The fire engine's engine is broken. It must be fixed before it can put out the fire.

What you do

- Provide the children with the role-play area.
- Observe the play. Use your professional judgement to decide when to introduce a new toy and play suggestion (intervention).
- Enter the play, introducing the new scenario, the damaged cars, or the fire engine.
- Withdraw from the play.

At the shops

Shopping is a part of everyday day life. Role-playing shops enables children to explore numeracy and develop vocabulary as they discuss goods. Children practise important language skills as they make decisions and requests.

What you need

- ✓ Shop area
- ✓ Table
- ✓ Till
- ✓ Items for sale (toy food, other toys, books, sun hats, sunglasses, party items)
- ✓ Money
- ✓ Price labels
- ✓ Shopping baskets
- ✓ Purses/wallets
- ✓ Teddy bears
- ✓ Holiday magazine

Interventions.

- There's going to be a party. What should you buy?
- Going on holiday. What do you need?
- Preparing for a teddy bears' picnic.

What you do

- Provide the children with the role-play area.
- Observe the play. Use your professional judgement to decide when to introduce a new toy and play suggestion (intervention).
- Enter the play, introducing the new scenario, the bears or magazine.
- Withdraw from the play.

Let's pretend!

At the doctor's

Children love to play doctors and nurses. Talking through play about sickness and injury helps to reassure children. Making toys better is very important!

What you need

- ✓ Bandages
- ✓ Stickers for plasters
- ✓ Toy stethoscope
- ✓ Toy thermometer
- ✓ Spoons for medicine
- ✓ Prescription pad and pencil
- ✓ Baby doll
- ✓ Small blankets
- ✓ White aprons and hats
- ✓ Doctors coats/ small white shirts
- ✓ Large bear
- ✓ A variety of dolls or animal toys

Interventions.

- The baby doll has chicken pox.
- Large bear has broken his leg.
- All the visiting toys have bad colds and need to be looked after.

What you do

- Provide the children with the role=play area.
- Observe the play. Use your professional judgement to decide when to introduce a new toy and play suggestion (intervention).
- Enter the play, introducing the new scenario, the poorly baby doll, injured bear or visiting sick toys.
- Withdraw from the play.

Language games

for chatty children and lovely listeners

Many early years games promote speaking and listening skills. Speaking and listening is at the heart of learning in the early years and the early years practitioner takes every opportunity to focus on developing those skills in his or her children, whatever the activity. In this section you will find toy-themed games that promote specific speaking and listening skills from sound discrimination to turn-taking skills.

Sound discrimination

The ability to discriminate between sounds is vital for clear speech production and comprehension. Children are exposed to all sorts of sounds: environmental sounds, speech sounds, musical sounds and animal sounds.

Environmental sounds

The world is full of sounds. Sometimes it's difficult to discriminate between different environmental sounds. Look around your setting and listen for the sounds that emerge when no one is talking.

You may hear:

- ✓ Chair legs scraping on the floor.
- ✓ Water running from the tap.
- ✓ The whirring of a computer.
- ✓ Sand being poured into a tray.
- ✓ Wheels of ride-on toys going round.
- ✓ Bricks being snapped and stacked.
- ✓ Crayons being dropped into a container.
- ✓ A felt pen writing on a whiteboard.

Try recording the sounds in your setting. Play the recording to the children and see if you can identify what is being played with.

Language games

The Toy Town band

Clapping hands, stamping feet and slapping knees are all ways of producing non-vocal sounds with the body. Games with body percussion can be lots of fun and children always enjoy them. Percussion instruments are readily available from toyshops or from educational suppliers. Drums, shakers, rattles and chimes can be made through junk play.

This activity encourages children to listen carefully to the sounds that you are making and reproduce them themselves. As you tell a story that is illustrated by percussion sound patterns the children repeat each of these sound patterns with their instruments and bodies.

What you do

- Seat the children with a toy on their lap.
- Hand out one shaker and bell stick each. Keep one for yourself.
- Explain to the children that you'd like to see if they can copy exactly what you do.
- Read the story, 'The Toy Town Parade' (page 60).
- Make sure the children lay the instruments on the floor when they are not using them — this will minimize any noisy fiddling!

What you need

- ✓ Shakers — one per child (small water bottles half filled with dried peas are ideal, but any shaker will do.)
- ✓ Tambourines / bell sticks — one per child
- ✓ Paper bag or scrunched up tissue paper
- ✓ Your bodies
- ✓ Soft toys — one per child, or pillow puppets (see page 14)

Links

CLL LfC. 30-50m

- Listen to others in one-to-one or small groups when conversation interests them.

CLL LfC. 40+m

- Speak clearly and audibly with confidence and control and show awareness of the listener. (ELG)

Section 6

The Toy Town parade

It was night time in Toy Land and all the toys were fast asleep.

Some of the toys were snoring!

(make snoring sound)

Soon it was morning. The sun rose in the sky.

The toys woke up and stretched.

(make yawning sound and stretch)

The toys were very excited because today was the day of the Toy Town Parade. But, oh no! It was raining!

(shake rattles gently)

Luckily the wind blew the clouds away

and the sun came out.

(make shh sound with mouths)

The toys had a breakfast of crunchy toast.

Munch, munch, munch

(rustle paper bags or scrunch tissue paper)

After breakfast the toys lined up in the town square.

They were ready to march and play their instruments.

Are you ready? 1 2 3 4

(bang and shake instruments, stamp feet)

Finally the toys finished the parade. What a brilliant parade it had been!

Links

CD CM&D. 30-50m

- Explore and learn how sounds can be changed.

CD CM&D. 40+m

- Explore the different sounds of instruments.

Where's teddy?

This game enables children to practise both listening to instructions and giving instructions. Practising instructional talk through play helps children to think logically and to put events in order.

What you need
✓ A small teddy

What you do

- Divide the children in to two groups – the finders and the tellers.

- Tell one group to shut their eyes, or if possible, take them into a different room.

- Hide the teddy in your setting, with the participation of the second group.

- Explain to the children that they must not tell the finders where the teddy is hiding.

- The teddy finders say the teddy finders rhyme.

Teddy bear, teddy bear
Where are you?
Teddy bear, teddy bear
please give us a clue!

- The tellers then tell the teddy finders to go forwards, backwards, up, down, or side to side until they find the hidden teddy.

- When the bear is found, swap groups.

Links

PSRN SS&M. 30-50m
- Observe and use positional language

PSRN SS&M. 40+m
- Find objects from positional or directional clues

Toy box lucky dip

This game encourages the use of descriptive language.

What you do

- Place the shredded newspaper into the box to create a lucky dip.
- Choose ten toys that will be hidden in the box.
- Seat the children in front of the box.
- Show the children each toy, making sure you name it.
- Place the toys in the box.
- Ask one child to be the 'dipper' and one child to be the 'guesser'.
- Blindfold the guesser.
- Ask the dipper to pick out a toy and describe it to the guesser.
- The guesser has three tries at guessing the toy.
- Repeat with other children.

What you need

- ✓ A large bucket or box
- ✓ Shredded newspaper
- ✓ A variety of toys

Links

PSED D&A. 40+m

- Maintain attention, concentrate and sit quietly when appropriate. (ELG)

CLL LfC. 40+m

- Speak clearly and audibly with confidence and control and show awareness of the listener. (ELG)

Toy talk

Young children are aware that all voices are not alike and are often adept at mimicking the voices of other people. They can imitate characters such as a giant's deep voice, a cow's mooing talk or a dinosaur's fierce roar. Play this game to explore other voice sounds and to imagine how toys would talk.

What you do

- Place the toys in the box.
- Seat the children and ask them to choose a toy.
- Pick a toy yourself.
- Explain to the children that in this game it is the toys that are talking. You are going to imagine their voices.
- Demonstrate with your toy. Ask your toy a simple question and answer in the toy's voice.
- Now ask the children's toys questions and see if they can answer on the toy's behalf.
- You could ask what their favourite food or game is.
- If a child is reluctant or shy, move on to another child.
- At the end of the game, allow the children to continue playing with their characters.

What you need

✓ A variety of toys – soft toy animals, plastic dinosaurs, action figure dolls
✓ A box

whisper whisper!

Links

CD CM&D. 30-50m
- Explore and learn how sounds can be changed.

CD DI&IP. 30-50m
- Engage in imaginative play and role-play based on own first hand experience.

Ride-on toys adventure trail

Play this game to practise positional language and have an exciting treasure hunting adventure. This is an outdoor or large space game.

What you do

- Set up your treasure trail.
- Look at your setting, indoors or outdoors and decide on the features you are going to use on your trail. Take photos of those objects.
- Stick the photos on a large piece of paper. This will be your map.
- Hide treasure around, under, or behind the features photographed.
- Choose children to play on your ride-on toys and explain that there is hidden treasure in the places that are photographed.
- Show them the map.
- Give the children a bucket each as they ride off on their treasure hunting adventure.
- Encourage the children to use positional language. Is it behind the plant pot? Is it under the mat? Is it on top of the bench?

What you need

✓ A camera
✓ Large piece of paper for a map
✓ Treasure - coins, jewels etc
✓ Buckets with handles

Links

PSRN SS&M. 30-50m

- Observe and use positional language.

PSRN SS&M. 40+m.

- Find items from positional or directional clues.